The CountryWise Guide To Skye

***'...the great changes in the life of the Highland people as written in the face of the land'.* -- I F Grant**

Castles and cottages, empty glens and bumps in the grass, all tell of people's lives and lifestyles. The CountryWise Guide introduces Skye's story. **The Landscape Story** tells you what to look out for and what it means. **The Tour** takes you round the island and points out features on the main roads and on some of the lesser roads and footpaths.

CONTENTS

N.B. For the footpath routes a good map is essential.

From Prehistory to 1263

Little is known about the daily lives of Skye people in the remote past. However, **Stone Age tombs** and **stone circle remains** show us that people of 5000 years ago were organised in communities and that they regarded funerals and other rituals as very important. Excavations show they were farmers growing grain and keeping cattle and sheep.

During the Iron Age around 2000 years ago, Skye people built **stone towers** known as *duns* or *brochs* around the coast and at important places inland. This suggests that by now the population had grown and people were having to compete for resources. Certainly the climate had worsened. When coast-watchers spotted enemy ships, it is thought that beacons were lit near the duns, sending warnings up and down the coast. This was the signal for herds to be hidden in the hills and for people to barricade themselves into the towers.

Skye was pleasantly wooded with deciduous trees such as oak and ash when the climate was at its best around 1000 BC. Climate change, tree-felling and extensive grazing have seen to it that only small areas of **ancient woodland** remain.

St Columba visited Skye about 585AD. The Irish monks who followed him set up churches. Their saintliness impressed so strongly that names of the places where they settled remain to this day even though Skye came under the rule of pagan Norwegian kings for 400 years from about 800 AD.

The Norwegians also left place names, of farms long since disappeared, and of **summer pastures** with names ending in *shader.* The Gaelic name for these was *airigh.* Every summer Skye farmers would take their herds of small highland cattle and sheep to these more distant pastures, and make their cheese and butter.

Much of Skye's past lies under grassy mounds, which are difficult to identify. Size, shape, position, silhouette, all give clues to identification.

Look for:

Stone Age tombs, chambered cairns
Crude stone chambers heaped over with stones, often grassed over.

Stone circle remains
Only isolated standing stones remain from the circles on Skye.

Stone towers, *duns* and *brochs*
Originally up to 13 metres high and 20 metres across. Brochs were circular, with double skinned walls containing chambers, stairs and passages within their thickness of 4-5m. There was a courtyard in the centre. Built of shaped stones without mortar and with one doorway, about 1metre high by 0.75metre wide.

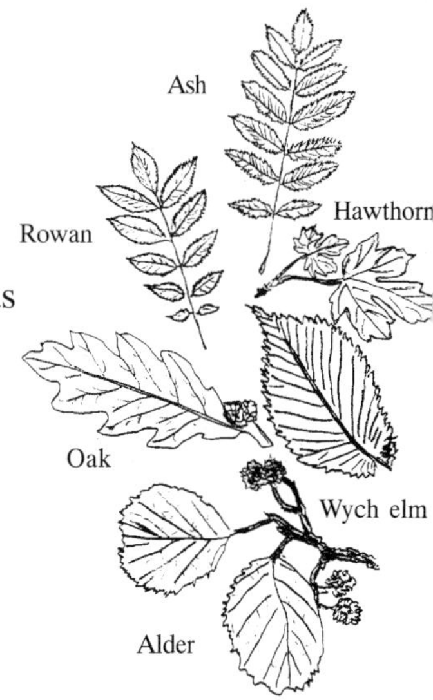

Ancient woodland
Small patches remain in sheltered areas. Boggy or heather-covered ground sometimes contains traces of prehistoric woodland from the time when the climate was warmer and dryer. In the 17th and 18th centuries oakwoods were coppiced i.e. harvested and allowed to regenerate from the stumps, sustainable crops for iron smelting.

Summer pastures, 'shielings'
They can be identified on maps by names ending in *shader* (Old Norse), or *airigh, airidh, ary,* (Gaelic).

The Clans, 1263 - 1745

The clans began as family groups who banded together for protection after Skye's overlord, the Norwegian king, was defeated, leaving a power vacuum, in 1263 . Clan chiefs fought each other for land and powèr. They rebuilt duns into medieval fortresses or built new ones, hence the seven **castles** of Skye.

The chief and the clan depended on each other. The clansfolk needed protection, the chief needed as many loyal warriors as possible. The chief administered the clan lands to maximise the numbers of warriors it could support. He was not concerned with financial income. He let estates to relatives who officered the war-band or provided skills in law, music or medicine. These tenants-in-chief let out farms to the clansfolk in return for labour services and produce.

The clansfolk lived in groups, up to twelve families sharing one farm. They lived close together in **townships,** clusters of one storey houses built of turf and stones. They were cattle-breeders, and lived well on the produce of their herds, lands and the sea.

Each family grew its own oats, rye, barley and flax on its share of unfenced strips of land, like the rest of medieval Europe. Where the soil was too thin to plough they worked it by hand. These strips were called *feannagan,* meaning unploughed, translated misleadingly as **lazy beds.** All animals were herded in common and sent away together to the Summer Pastures.

Inter-clan fighting was stopped by King James VI in 1601 (he was concerned about his chances of succeeding to the English throne). His "Regulations for Chiefs" insisted on their attendance at court and an education in English, not Gaelic, for their children.

This lifestyle demanded cash, not personal loyalty. As the chiefs no longer depended on the goodwill of the warriors of the clan, they were able to demand rents in cash to finance their new and expensive lifestyle. Their tenants-in-chief developed the cattle trade, and by the end of the 1600s, thousands of shaggy black highland cattle met up in the local fairs held on the **cattle stances** to begin a 600 mile walk to the fattening marshes of Norfolk en route for the dining tables of London.

With rent to pay, the living standards of the clansfolk dropped. They dropped meat from their diet, their beasts going to finance their rents. There was no surplus money for building substantial houses or churches. These survive only as **ruins.**

Look for:

Castles

Strongholds of the clan chief or his deputy and focus of clan loyalty, lawgiving, and Gaelic music and verse. Staff included bodyguards, horsemen, and a man whose duty was to carry the chief through rivers and into boats. Most important were the warriors' athletic games, trials of strength and skill, the ancestors of today's Highland Games.

Lazy beds

Cultivation strips 2m wide, 2-200metres long, they look like stranded whales. Built up with seaweed and soot-rich thatch which was stripped from the houses annually. The main crop was oats, later, potatoes. Lazy beds were worked with the *caschrom,* the foot plough. With this a man could "plough" a quarter of an acre per day. Lazy beds were used into modern times.

Townships

The townships were higgledy-piggledy groups of houses built close together, unlike the later crofting townships with their individual 2-4 acre plots.

Cattle stances

Cattle markets, often on rich lochside grazings.

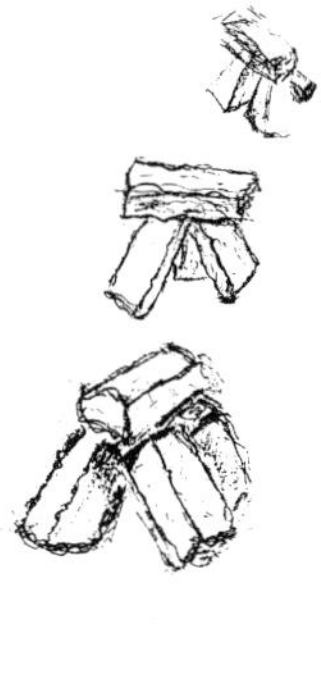

Peat cuttings

Lack of trees meant using peat for heating and cooking. Peat is compacted vegetation which cannot rot down because it is too wet and cold for microbial action. A family needed 15,000 peats per year; a man can cut 1000 per day. After cutting they dry by the trench before being carted home.

Churches

The only public buildings. Cattle-dealers up from the south in April and May would give notice here as to when and where they would be buying stock.

The Landlords, 1745 - 1886

After the scare of the 1745 Rebellion, the government abolished the chiefs' remaining powers of law and justice and encouraged them to join the English aristocracy. The chiefs were left with the clan lands but without clan responsibilities - and with increased expenses now they had joined a consumer society.

They raised rents, driving some tenants-in-chief to emigrate to America taking farming capital and subtenants with them. Depopulation loomed. From 1803-1821 the government subsidised the building of a road network in Scotland to stimulate industry. Skye's **first roads** appeared, to assist the export of cattle.

The chiefs, now thorough-going landlords, perceived that they could more fully exploit their estates' resources in view of the boom prices of the Napoleonic wars, around 1800, if they reorganised. They created large farms from the communal self-subsistence farms and resettled dispossessed families on individual allotments, *crofts,* and channelled them into wage-earning, by fishing and kelp-making, to pay the rent. (*Kelp* - seaweed ash, an industrial alkali for glass and soap). **Crofting townships** were laid out on the poorer land along the coast. The better land was enclosed in part with **stone walls** and provided with handsome **farmhouses** for the new class of farmers working for profits.

The population rose. Family crofts were subdivided into tiny holdings. But the kelp market crashed and the fishing was unsuccessful. The common diet all over Skye was simply potatoes and fish, and for some months of the year just shellfish. When the harvests failed in the 1830's and 1840's, people starved . Landlords faced bankruptcy as rents went unpaid. They carried out **clearances** of remaining family farmers to create high rent **sheep ranches.** Those evicted were forced to emigrate or to crowd into congested crofting townships where ten families might share land formerly occupied by one.

Crofters' grazing and other rights such as taking heather for thatching were whittled away to maximise resources for the new **sporting lodges.** These became the chief source of estate income in the agricultural depression from the 1870s which resulted from cheap wool and mutton imports from Australia. Crofters' rent strikes and violent demonstrations, gleefully reported as 'The Crofters' War' by the London popular press, led to an enquiry and to the Crofters' Act of 1886, the first of several to improve the crofters' position.

Look for:

Crofting townships

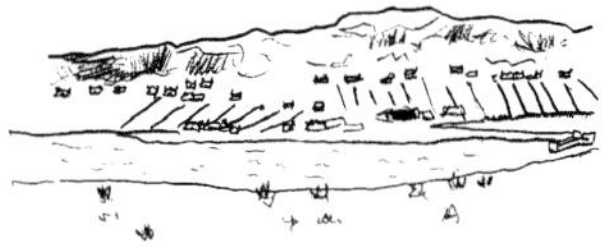

Individual allotments, crofts, usually of 2-4 acres, were laid out in planned settlements. Crofters built their own houses and grew their own food. The original houses have been rebuilt. They were longhouses with an entrance through a small cow byre where manure was nearly 1 metre thick by spring. The living area had a peat fire smouldering on an open hearth. Fish dried in the smoke above. Clothes, shoes, ropes, tools, fishnets, were homemade.

Kelp kilns

Walled trenches dug by the shore to burn seaweed into potash, used in manufacturing glass and soap.

Farmhouses, stone walls

Built by landlords to attract the new kind of farmer tenant with capital and "modern" techniques. Enclosures enabled tenants to improve land with lime and fertilizers.

Churches of the Free Church of Scotland

Crofters felt the hardships of the 1830s would be eased if landlords would release more land for crofters but landlords and the Church of Scotland supported emigration. Crofters wanted the right to choose sympathetic ministers. The Free Church was born in 1843. For years landlords refused land for radical churches. The Free Church helped to weld supporters of land reform into an articulate group which eventually achieved success.

Skye's road system

Supervised by the great engineer Thomas Telford who was dedicated to the idea of improving the lot of his fellow Scots. Some of the fine early bridges are now bypassed and can be admired free of traffic.

Sporting lodges

Luxury houses for sporting house-parties, shooting stags and grouse, salmon-fishing. The leisure industry begins.

Modern Times, 1886 - Present Day

The Crofters' War led to the Crofters' Act of 1886 which gave crofters security of tenure, and compensation if, for example, they built or improved houses or drained their land. So the old so-called *black houses* - of rough stone - gradually went out in favour of **dressed stone houses** with slate roofs, many built with government assistance.

Crofters' demand for land, born of a traditional belief that all had rights in clan lands, was finally satisfied when the government bought up estates before and after the 1914-1918 war, and broke up the large sheep farms to enlarge old crofts and create new ones.

Since then support in the form of state benefits and European Community grants has changed the crofters' lifestyle. From smallholding with a part-time job it has become stockrearing combined with a full-time job. Small-scale crop growing is redundant - croft "aprons" are now down to grass, and contractors cut the grass for sileage and bale it in black plastic.

There are jobs in the state service sector, and a handful in **forestry, farming, fish-farming** and **quarrying. Shell-fishing** has been very successful in recent years. But the biggest development is in tourism. **Houses and bungalows** have gone up with grants for bed-and-breakfast businesses. **Hotels** and **hostels** have been built and enlarged. Telford's **roads** have been widened and upgraded - and fenced in places to save sheep from faster, more frequent traffic.

Skye's people still make a living from the land but, as with so many areas of marginal agriculture and outstanding beauty, less of it derives from produce and more from the visitors who come for the scenery. And the scenery can be a double pleasure, enjoyed twice over, - for its beauty, which is magical, and for the signs of what I F Grant called

'...the great changes in the life of the Highland people as written in the face of the land'.

Look for:

Crofters' first permanent houses
One storey, with chimneys. Together with the dormer (storm) window plan, these mushroomed when loans under the Crofters' Housing Scheme took off in the 1920s. Both types look thoroughly traditional but are not actually all that old.

LODGEPOLE PINE

SITKA SPRUCE

Forestry
The Forestry Commission is the biggest forestry enterprise on Skye. It is managed on behalf of us all, balancing public access with production. It began in 1932, planting for strategic reserves, but from 1938 social and economic benefits for depopulated areas were an important consideration.

The two species mainly used are Sitka spruce and Lodgepole pine. As new plantations grow, the habitat and therefore the bird population changes. Moorland species give way to thicket, light woodland, and finally to forest species.

Fish-farming cages
In many sea lochs. They house young salmon from two to four years. The first two years are spent in freshwater nurseries.

Fishing ports
Home to two-men boats fishing for prawns, lobsters and crabs.

Roads
Being upgraded all the time. Travel the minor non-professional, non-Telford roads, to deepen appreciation of the wildness of the country, the loop road to Ord in Sleat for example.

SOUTH

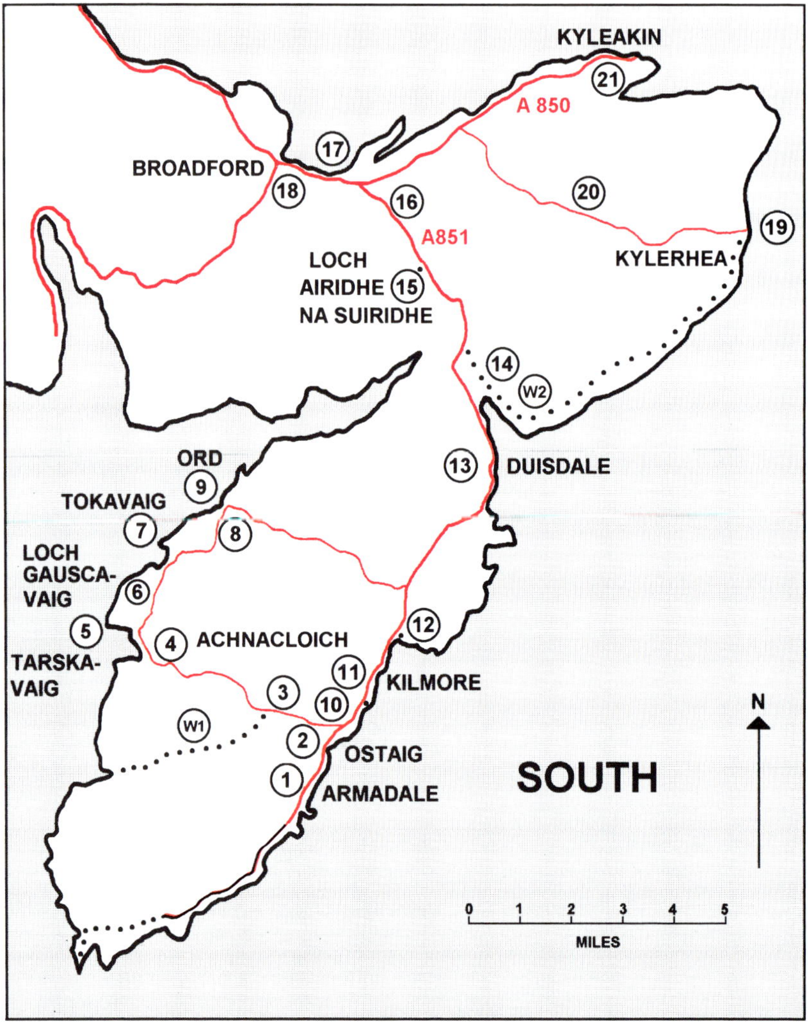

Scenery: This is the Sleat Peninsula where rough pasture blankets the low mountains of the interior and the coastline is fringed with crofting settlements. Amazing views to the mainland mountains to the west, legendary sunsets over the Cuillins to the east.

W1. Walk to Dalavil Glen, planted about 1800, and Caradal township, abandoned around 1880, 8 miles return.

W2. Kinloch to ancient woodland beside Loch na Dal, 1-2 miles one way.

Landscape story: The clansfolk as elsewhere on Skye were subsistence cattle farmers. They farmed communally with perhaps 12 families sharing one farm. The farms were arranged around the peninsula each having a wedge of territory that reached from the sea through the arable land to the hill grazings and thus a share in each of the different resources.

Two great clan fortresses guarded these lands, Dunscaig on the west, Knock on the east. Many a tale of treachery and savage revenge lingers round these gaunt ruins. In 1800 the MacDonald chief - as landlord - replanned his estates to exploit more fully the resources of land and sea. Clansfolk were cleared off the joint farms to became individual tenants, *crofters,* on smallholdings, *crofts,* growing their own food and paying the rent from wages earned in the landlord's enterprises. This is why the landscape today is largely crofting townships. The occasional big farmhouse was built for the 'improved' farms which Lord MacDonald created from the best land and let to big farmers who used new techniques.

1. CLANDONALD CENTRE

.Here are the landscaped ruins of the former Armadale Castle, built around 1815 for the 18th chief of the Clan MacDonald who at one time owned more than half the island. The exhibitions give a feel of the power and kinship ties which were the Scottish clan system. The views from the beautiful wooded gardens and across the sea to the mainland mountains of Knoydart are superb, even by Skye standards.

Americans, Canadians, Australians and New Zealanders drop into the Centre's library to find out about their local ancestors.

Lord MacDonald who laid out these gardens, built the castle, and the grand **stables** which are now a shop and restaurant, was responsible for much of the scenery of this part of Skye as you see it today. He laid out the crofting townships, instigated the building of the road to Broadford, planted woodland, and built the solid Georgian farmhouses, as part of his big reorganisation of the estates between 1800 and 1825.

2. UPPER OSTAIG (EAST BAY)

Large house built for a modern farmer around 1820 when the estate was phasing out farms worked communally, by small self-sufficient tenants, in favour of large scale enterprises farmed for profit. Ostaig's farm buildings, the *steadings,* were further up the road.

3. LAZY BEDS

Up the loop road at 0.9 miles from the junction, by the sheep pens, the *fank,* improved with European Community money, the road here cuts through grassed-over **lazy beds,** old strip cultivation which was once part of the arable lands of the cleared farm of Linigary.

W1. Dalavil Glen and Caradal. 8 miles return. Map advisable.

At 1.8 miles from the junction. Leave cars just off the road. There is a good track as far as the glen. The **canal** joining the loch to the sea was built to encourage salmon to the loch and to drain the land nearby. **Dalavil woods,** mixed woodland replanted by the estate c1800, with some old beeches remaining. **Caradal township ruins,** partly abandoned, partly cleared around 1880.

4. ACHNACLOICH (STONEFIELD)

Crofting township laid out in 1811 with 14 allotments, *crofts,* running in an arc from the sea, across where the road is now, and along the hillside. The best view of the surveyor's layout is from the north end where you can see the 'aprons' of croft allotments stretching down the hill. The original settlers had to build their own houses - drystone, thatched, with the cow byre at the entrance end. The crofts varied between 2-4 acres each.

5. TARSKAVAIG (COD BAY).

Crofting township. Under the old communal farm system there were 4 families on this farm. In 1811 it was laid out with 31 crofts of 2-4 acres. By 1883 the crofts had been subdivided to accommodate 40 families, some of whom had been cleared from land made over to sheep farming. Ruins of the early drystone cottages can be seen, also the one and two storey cottages which became popular following security of tenure which was granted in 1886. The Crofters' Housing Scheme played a big part by making available plans and materials for the one storey plan in 1920 and for the two storey plan in 1929.

6. LAZY BEDS AND PEAT CUTTINGS BY LOCH GAUSCAVAIG

The road again cuts through an old patch of **Lazy Beds**. Large old **Peat Cutting** on the east side of the road.

7. TOKAVAIG (ROUGH BAY)

Crofting township laid out in 1811 originally with only 7 crofts, of 8-30 acres each. **Dunscaith Castle**. Site of a prehistoric fortress or *Dun,* which became a medieval stronghold of the Macleods, and then the residence of the chiefs of the MacDonalds. They left it soon after 1600 to live at Duntulm Castle in the north, where they had acquired further estates.

In the 1500's, so the story goes, the chief's cousin arrived to find the household entertaining the chief's wife's relations. Cousin Ronald was so angered by their arrogance that in the night he secretly murdered twelve of them and slung their bodies where the hostess would see them from her window the next day. The chief could not understand why his guest took his leave so early in the morning.

8. GROVE OF THE DRUIDS AT COILLE THOCABHAIG (TOKAVAIG WOOD)

A National Nature Reserve,this is one of the very few remaining parts of Skye's **ancient woodland,** with oak, ash, birch, and hazel. Part has been managed as oak standards with hazel coppice (poles cut at ground level). The name may indicate a place of pagan worship. Echoes of the high moral esteem in which the Druids were held lingered on in Gaelic folklore: 'Though near is stone to earth, nearer than that is the help of the Druid.'

9. ORD (ROUND HILL)

Ord House. Down the side road. Built in the 1820s by Lord Alexander MacDonald for the new single tenant farm of 5-6000 acres carved out of the old common lands. A candle in the sea-facing room is said to have served to guide smugglers running wine from Bordeaux. The first tenant took a patriarchal attitude to the cottars (landless labourers) he found living on his new farm. He allowed them a few acres and a house rent free in return for labour services when needed - harvesting, haymaking, boat repairs - a hangover from Clan/medieval times.

St Comgan's chapel, *Teampull Chaon,* 8th century. Ruins under a grassy mound with fine views over the coast and islands. St Comgan was one of a number of missionaries, many of them Irish, who set up chapels in early medieval Skye. To find St Comgan's chapel, take the side road above the shore and in 130 yards or so turn right through a stile.

10. SABHAL MOR OSTAIG (THE BIG BARN OF OSTAIG)

The **Gaelic college,** brainchild of the landowner Sir Iain Noble who bought half of the MacDonald estate in Sleat. The college offers courses in business and computing and the media, and in the Gaelic language, music and folklore. The older buildings at the back were the **steadings** for Upper Ostaig. The steadings' high quality masonry would have contrasted strongly with the crofters' houses of the time which were still home-built of drystone with thatched roofs.

11. KILMORE (PRINCIPAL CHURCH)

Manse, up a drive on the west, built about 1815, a gothic mini-castle for the minister, to match Armadale castle, by the same architect, Gillespie Graham. On the east, **Parish church** of Sleat and burial place of the MacDonald chiefs. **Ruins** of the previous church in the graveyard where in 1746 the 15th McDonald chief was buried with unprecedented grandeur. In those days of the Clans funerals were customarily occasions for drinking beforehand at the house and again at the graveside which often sparked old disagreements into fighting On this occasion, 'three men were killed and 50 taken out of the church yard with the breath just left in them'.

12. KNOCK (HILL)

Castle Knock, or Castle Camus, *Castle of the Hill or Bay.* Leave cars on the road. One of the two great fortresses of Sleat. When the MacDonald of the day refused to recognise William of Orange as the new king in 1689 government troops arrived by sea, rowed ashore, and burned down MacDonald's house in Armadale. Subsequently they had to retreat to this castle which was then unoccupied but were forced to surrender and were hanged from makeshift gallows made of oars. **Knock farm.** Built in 1825 using stones from the castle.

13. DUISDALE (MISTY DALE)

The land here was held by the MacKinnons in return for service as standard bearers to the MacDonalds. **Free Church and Manse.** Built in 1859 by which time the Free Church founded by anti-landlord radicals in1843 had become more acceptable to the MacDonalds. To begin with the MacDonalds had refused to allow Free Churches to be built on their estates and turned out some of the Free church members. **Duisdale House,** now a hotel, was a MacKinnon shooting lodge built in 1876, for which four crofts were cleared. A fifth was turned into the gamekeeper's cottage.

14. KINLOCH (HEAD OF THE LOCH)

Kinloch Lodge. Former MacDonald shooting lodge, now a hotel and home of the present Lord and Lady MacDonald. **Lazy beds** by the road just opposite the Lodge are reminders of the times when people of necessity grew their own food and went hungry when bad weather destroyed the harvest. These tiny beds were fertilized with seawood and grew potatoes, the staple food.

W2. Kinloch to Coille Leitir Fura, ancient oak woodland
1-2 miles one way, forestry track.

15. LOCH AIRIDHE NA SUIRIDHE (LOCH OF THE SHIELING OF COURTSHIP)

The river and a bridge here were also named after this *shieling* (summer grazing place) where the young women would come to live in the shieling huts for six weeks in May and June to tend the milking cattle and make the butter and cheese for the winter. Some of the loveliest lyrics in the gaelic language celebrate this happy season.

Shielings were used all over Europe in the cattle districts. You can find them still in use in, for example, Switzerland. The same type of plunger butter churn as was used on Skye is found also as far away as Norway and the mountains of north Spain.

16. MARKET STANCE

Where the pylons cross the road. **Market and resting place** for the black highland cattle, Skye's chief industry during the Clan period and the beginning of the Landlord period until about 1820. The beasts from Sleat and the shores of Loch Eishort would here join with the droves from north Skye and the Outer Hebrides on their way to swim the dangerous crossing at Kylerhea, just the beginning of their 700 mile walk to the dining tables of London.

17. WATERLOO

Crofting township signposted just outside Broadford, which was settled by veterans of that battle in which 1,600 Skyemen took part. Apart from cattle the chief product of Skye during the 18th and early 19th centuries was people, i.e. emigrants and fighting men. A rising population coupled with poor employment and a long standing fighting tradition - the last inter-clan battle in Skye took place as late as 1601 - led to 10,000 men enlisting in the 40 years up to 1837. (The present population of Skye is only around 9000).

18. BROADFORD

Once a crofting township, now a **local centre** for services and tourism. **Liveras chambered cairn,** a prehistoric tomb overgrown with trees and wild raspberries. To find it take the road signed 'hospital' (A854) for 0.2 mile. It is on the left, between two houses. **Skye Environmental Centre** for information and publications about Skye.

19. KYLERHEA

The most atmospheric arrival point in Skye. For 300 years this was the crossing place for the cattle droves, formerly the wealth of Skye. The beasts swam across at slack tide tied nose to tail in a line of five held by a man in the stern of a rowing boat. Rowing was one of the services expected from his clansmen by his superior in return for farmland. The scenery to Broadford is wild and empty, up the pass and down through Glen Arroch. The road is still largely and attractively single track, a route to savour, not to hurry through.

On the mainland slipway are the cobbles that helped the highland cattle struggle on shore after their swim from Skye.

20. ROAD

This **road,** finished in 1813, was, not surprisingly, the most difficult section of all Skye's first roads.The roads were built chiefly to facilitate the rearing and sale of the black cattle which were the chief wealth of Skye. The landlords and the government shared the cost of £400 per mile.

21. KYLEAKIN (THE STRAITS OF HAAKON)

70 - 80 forts once ringed the coastline to protect the inhabitants from seaborne raiders. As you approach Kyleakin you can see the remains of one of them, **Castle Maol,** *(Castle on the Headland)* **also called Dun Akyn** (*Fort Haakon).* Haakon was the last of the Norwegian overlords of Skye. His warships passed this way in 1263 on their way to defeat in the battle which ended 400 years of Norse domination, and began the reign of local warlords, i.e. the clan chiefs.

Dun Akyn was the site of a prehistoric fort *(dun* means fort), and after that, a medieval castle, the home of a Norwegian princess, Saucy Mary, married to a MacDonald. Legend tells she stretched a chain across the straits in order to levy tolls on passing shipping. Later the castle was held for the MacDonalds by the Clan MacKinnon whose lands stretched like a sandwich filling between those of the powerful clans of MacLeod in the north and MacDonald in the south.

CENTRAL

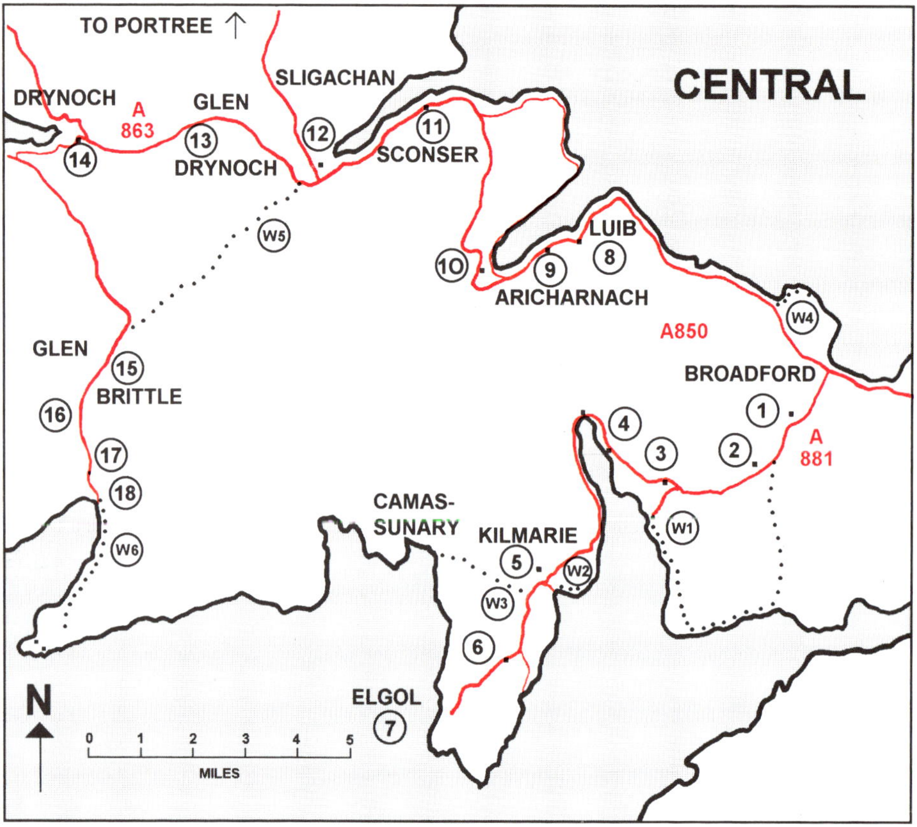

BROADFORD - ELGOL

Scenery: *Empty moorland, crofting hamlets, views of Blaven and the Cuillins, fishing/crofting port of Elgol, renowned for sunsets.*

Special interest: Summer boat trips from Elgol to Loch Coruisk, weather permitting.

W1. Walk from Kilbride to the cleared townships of Suishnish and Boreraig on the coast, 9 miles return or 13 returning through the hills.

W2. Walk from Kilmarie to the old shielings at Camuasunary, 5 miles return. W3. Kilmaree to Dun Ringill, 1 mile one way.

.**Landscape story:** This is the parish of Strath, MacKinnon country, and as in the rest of Skye cattle breeding was the predominating activity. The MacKinnons were the third great clan of Skye and their lands stretched from Elgol in the southwest to Kyleakin in the east. They had to sell in 1765. In 1851 the owner of Strathaird, the western part, bargained with the inhabitants who were in arrears with their rent, and as a result cleared 500 people from 8 townships to free the land for sheep. Prehistoric tombs and forts.

1. CHAMBERED CAIRN

Now mostly covered with grass, 1.4 miles from the junction with the Broadford road.

2. CILCHRIOSD (CHRIST'S CHURCH)

Former parish church of Strath, in ruins since 1838 and burial place of the MacKinnons. As the church was the only public building the cattle-dealers from the south arriving in late April and May would give notice here as to where and when they would be ready to purchase cattle.

3. KILBRIDE (ST BRIDGET'S CHURCH)

Large farmhouse amongst trees, used as the manse in the 1840s when the minister customarily lived on his glebe farm. The minister's friend was out walking one day in 1853 and witnessed the exodus of the evicted communities of Boreraig and Suishnish:

'I could see that the minister with his wife and daughters had come out to meet the people and bid them all farewell...Everyone was in tears..When they set off once more a cry of grief went up to heaven....and after the last of the emigrants had disappeared behind the hill, the sound seemed to re-echo through the whole wide valley of Strath in one prolonged note of desolation'.

W1. Walk from Kilbride to Suishnish and Boreraig
Leave cars at the coast and walk the landrover track to its end at Suishnish. A footpath skirts the sheep enclosures and continues along to Boreraig as a rough path. There are many ruins here. The two townships became one sheep farm.

4. TORRIN (MOUNDS)

Lazy beds at the end of the village by Loch Slapin. At the loch head a **bridge** with the 12 stars of the European Community. Purely functional without the least aesthetic pretensions.

5. KILMARIE (ST MAOLRUBHA'S CHURCH)

W2. Walk to Dun Ringill, traditionally the stronghold of the Mackinnons, which is reached from the ornamental bridge near Kilmarie House. Park, preferably, in Kilmarie.
W3. Walk to Camasunary (Bay of the Fair Shielings). Land-rover track all the way .

6. LAZY BEDS

Half a mile on from the side road to Drinan, a big patch of **lazy beds** reaching down to the river.

7. ELGOL (HOLY HILL)

400 people are said to have crowded into Elgol at the time of the clearances. Today, small **local boats** catch lobsters, crabs, and prawns which go via Inverness to Spain.

BROADFORD - SLIGACHAN - DRYNOCH - GLEN BRITTLE

Scenery: *Broadford - Sligachan, coastal views, small crofting townships; at Sligachan - Drynoch, Cuillin mountains and empty valley; Glen Brittle, peaceful river valley, forestry; island views.*

Landscape story: Along the coast from Aricharnach to Sligachan, clearances of crofting townships around 1850 to enlarge the MacDonald deer forest. From Sligachan inland is MacLeod country, the parish of Bracadale which was virtually all cleared to create just six sheep farms around 1850.

W4. Forestry walk along the coast with superb views to Raasay and Scalpay. Parking and picnic site.

W5. Walk from Sligachan to Glen Brittle, 5 miles one way.

W6. From Glen Brittle, a walk along the coast to Rubh an Dunain chambered cairn and dun, 5-6 miles return. Allow 4 hours.

8. LUIB (THE BENDS)

Folk museum. A cottage which 'depicts living conditions in the late 19th century'. Peat fire, tools and furniture. Note the Skye dresser: because of leaks in the thatch, Skye dressers stored the plates sloping forwards instead of backwards so any tarry drips would fall on the back of the plates. **Loch Ainort Fish Farms.** Fish cages in the loch hold growing salmon 2 - 4 years old. The first two years are spent in freshwater.

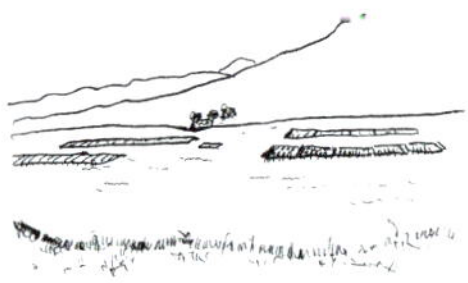

9. ARICHARNACH (THE SHIELINGS IN THE STONY FIELD)

Only a few houses now, Aricharnoch was cleared in 1853 to enlarge Lord Macdonald's deer forest of Sconser.

10. HEAD OF THE LOCH

Cattle stance where the droves of black cattle from the north of Skye and the Outer Hebrides would rest on their way south. Along the old coast road, **Moll,** also cleared for the Sconser deer forest. Worth a detour for the island views.

11. SCONSER

Sconser Lodge Hotel, formerly Lord MacDonald's shooting lodge. The **nine-hole golf** course next door lies over the township of Torramichaig, also cleared in 1853.

12. SLIGACHAN (SHELLY PLACE)

Sligachan Hotel. From here the Cuillins were first conquered by those Victorian pioneers whose photographs are displayed inside. Sligachan lies at the hub of routes through the mountains. Cattle from the grazings by Loch Bracadale and the glens north of the Cuillins gathered at the **cattle stance** by the campsite, where you can see the **ruins of the early inn,** which was used by the drovers.

W4. Walk to Glen Brittle. A clearly-defined path leads over open moorland. At the top of the pass on the left is Coire na Creiche (Corry of the Cattle) where MacLeods on a cattle rustling expedition had collected up cattle seized from herds from many miles around. They were preparing to return home with their booty when they were overtaken by the MacDonalds, who took their revenge. It happened in 1601, part of the dispute known as the War of the One-eyed Woman which followed the humiliation of a Macdonald bride. This was the last inter-clan battle before King James VI brokered a lasting peace using the clan lands as security.

13. GLENDRYNOCH (VALLEY OF THORNS

Cleared for sheep around 1850. The odd patch of **lazy beds** shows where people once lived.

14. DRYNOCH (PLACE OF THORNS)

The most impressive and extensive series of **Lazy Beds.** Pause at the road junction and see them all around. Opposite, the slopes of Satran are hung with strips some only a few metres long, others 150 metres or more. Away to the right another set slopes steeply down to Loch Harport. There are many more. The hillsides would have been swarming with people at potato-planting time, carrying up creels of seaweed to manure the beds, turning over the soil with the *caschrom,* the traditional foot plough.

15. GLEN BRITTLE

Forestry Commision's first estate on Skye. Trees planted in the 1930s are now mature. Replanting is planned to include more native deciduous species to add variety and colour and will follow the contours instead of having ruler-straight plantation boundaries.

16. Ruined township. Where river and road come close together, there are house ruins disposed in the higgledy-piggledy cluster typical of the old clan townships. Picture these cottages, peat smoke seeping through the chimney-less thatched roofs, and everywhere the reek of cattle dung. The cattle which were overwintered in the byres were sometimes so emaciated by the spring that they had to be carried out to the spring pasture. Nearby are the **Lazy Beds** where the township's potatoes were grown.

17. Glenbrittle House, built for the sheep farm which comprised the whole of the glen.

18. THE COAST

Parking. There are **lazy beds** on the hill above the camp site.

W6. South along the coast to Rubh an Dunan, a chambered cairn, the best example on Skye, and a dun. Take the track along the coast southwards from the camp site. It deteriorates to a rough path. 2 miles from camp it turns inland. Lazy beds here. Keep up along the contour parallel with the old wall on the other side of the small valley. Cross where a wide swath of green runs up hillside from wall. Follow it up. When the loch comes into view, the cairn is near its shore on the right, the dun is by the coast on the left. Map essential.

NORTH WEST

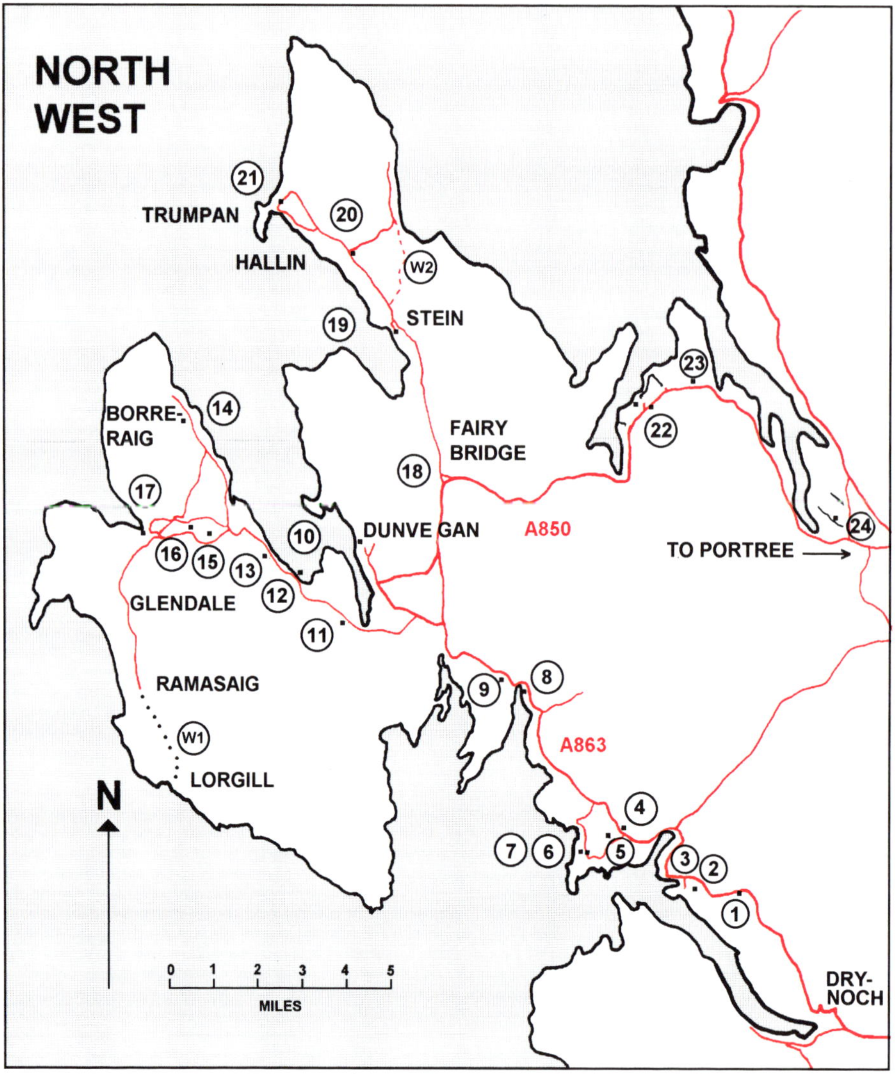
NORTH
WEST
21
TRUMPAN
20
HALLIN
W2
19
STEIN
BORRE-
RAIG
14
23
22
FAIRY
BRIDGE
18
17
10
DUNVE GAN
A850
24
TO PORTREE
16
15
13
GLENDALE
12
11
9
8
RAMASAIG
W1
A863
LORGILL
N
4
7
6
5
3
2
1
0 1 2 3 4 5
MILES
DRY-
NOCH

DRYNOCH - DUNVEGAN

Scenery: *Can seem a little desolate, with views of the strange vertical cliffs and plateaux of MacLeod's Tables, the 59 million-years-old volcanic basalt rock formations.*

Landscape story. The Stone and Iron Age people left many traces here, chambered cairns, duns, brochs and underground houses. This is MacLeod country since medieval times. The parish of Bracadale which makes up most of the route to Dunvegan was almost entirely cleared to create six sheep farms around 1850. Most of it was acquired by the Board of Agriculture in 1920 to break up into crofts and resettle land-hungry ex-servicemen. Some areas have been sold off for farms, for example Gesto and Glendrynoch.

1. COAST ROAD BY LOCH HARPORT (LOCH BY THE GOAT FIORD)

The two rivers you cross, the Meadale and the Sumerdale, gave their names to medieval farms (*dale*-field, Old Norse). Townships containing 22 familes were cleared off for sheep around 1850. **Lazy beds,** notably by the bridge over the Sumardale river.

2. DUN TAIMH

A short stiff climb and not much to see when you reach the top apart from the cairn built to commemorate Queen Victoria's Jubilee. But a splendid viewpoint out to the islands.

3. SIDE ROAD TO GESTO

Gesto, for centuries held by senior members of the MacLeod clan, was in the 1600s the home of Do'ull MacIain ic Sheamuis, the man who pioneered the cattle trade to the mainland which became Skye's chief source of wealth. As a young man he had distinguished himself in the last inter-clan battle in Skye, during the War of the One-eyed Woman, so his career spanned the change from the old clan cattle-raiding days to peaceable times and the beginning of the trading economy.

4. DUN BEAG (SMALL FORT)

The best example of a broch on Skye. The walls still stand to a height of several metres with chambers, stairs and upper passages. There is a good explanation board and picnic area.

5. ULLINISH (ULLI'S POINT)

On the corner of the side road to Ullinish is the hill called **Knoc Ullinish,** *Hill of Strife,* a Moot Hill where the chief and his advisors would sit in judgement.

On the flanks of Knoc Ullinish is a prehistoric underground house, a ***souterrain,*** used to safeguard people and goods c200AD. To find it, go 0.3 mile down the Ullinish turn. Walk across to the foot of the hill keeping to the right across the old lazy beds. Cross two tumbledown walls and you are there.

6. Less than a mile from the souterrain, **Ullinish Lodge Hotel** built as the principal house for a clan estate it later became a MacLeod shooting lodge and is now a hotel. 7. Just to the north of it, by the road, is a much-robbed skeletal **chambered cairn.**

8. CAROY (RED ROCK)

St John's chapel. Rebuilt because the MacLeod of Gesto shot a seal on a Sunday (was it ruining the fishing?) and thus incurred the disapproval of the parish church's congregation. These were zealots who refused to partake of communion with those whose behaviour they disapproved of, and whose views were to lead to the setting up of the Free Church a few years later. MacLeod restored this old Episcopal (High Church) Chapel and worshipped here instead. It lies off a part of the old road, now a layby, and being shrouded in trees is easily overlooked. A beautiful and tranquil burial ground, overlooked by the great prehistoric tombs which dominate the skyline to the north.

9. CHAMBERED CAIRNS

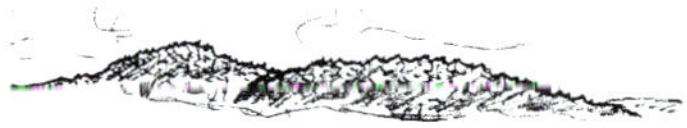

These two prehistoric tombs dominate the approach from the south.

10. DUNVEGAN (FORT OF THE FEW)

Dunvegan Castle. Still the home of the chief of the Clan MacLeod. In clan times he could deal out a death sentence, bestow estates, and claim dues such as the best horse of a deceased tenant. Exhibitions, gardens, woodland.

DUNVEGAN - GLENDALE

***Scenery:** Mountains, sea lochs, crofting townships.*

W1. Easy walk along a track from Ramasaig to the cleared township of Lorgill, 1.5 miles.

Landscape story: Crofting townships, which were laid out about 1811to exploit the fishing which was not successful, and the kelp. The settlers had been dispossessed from areas cleared for big sheep farms. Around 3000 acres of arable land in the parish were put down to pasture from arable between the 1790s and 1840, causing immense hardship. In 1840 the minister reported that many people lived mainly on shellfish for part of the year. In 1905, with government help, Glendale became the first estate to be jointly owned by the crofters themselves.

11. DUN OSDALE (VALLEY OF THE RIVER'S MOUTH)

Perched on the knoll overlooking the turn to Uiginish.

12. SKINIDIN (DUN OF THE WITHERED GRASS)

Opposite the house with the post box are two tiny islands with a **kelp kiln** and a seaweed-drying area. The kelp industry, seaweed ash, was extremely profitable for the landlords during the Napoleonic wars until 1825.

13. COLBOST (COLD FARM)

Folk Museum. 'The Museum contains implements and furniture of bygone days, has a peat fire burning ... and is typical of living conditions in the 19th century'. Earth floor and central fire open to the roof thatch. When the woman of the house had to fetch peats for the fire the toddlers, for safety, were tethered up or put in a barrel.

14. BORRERAIG (FORTRESS BAY)

Piping Museum. The land round here was held by the MacCrimmons for generations, in return for services as the MacLeods' (bag)pipers. The MacCrimmons ran a famous college of piping which sent its pupils practising on the hills nearby.

15. CAIRN, GLENDALE MARTYRS

They did not meet an unpleasant death but suffered 61 days imprisonment for their part in the fight for a more equitable share of the land. Crofters from the area applied for the lease of the farm of Waterstein and were rejected. Some of them were living on tiny crofts of land reduced some years previously from 6 to 3 acres and now the new estate owner barred them from keeping sheep dogs (bad for the grouse) and gathering driftwood.

They went on rent strike, drove their stock on to Waterstein, and beat up the estate shepherds, and later, a corps of police. The government sent a gunboat with an investigator, Malcolm MacNeil. The London press whipped up much public sympathy. There had been fighting over land rights elsewhere on Skye and the situation was known as 'The Crofters' War'. The “Martyrs” got 61 days but the report was sympathetic to them. In 1905 the government enabled the crofters to buy the estate freehold over a 50 year period, giving independence to crofters for the first time.

16. VIEWPOINT

At the top of the pass. A splendid view of the crofting townships which make up Glendale. Pooltiel loch where the gunboat arrived, Upper and Lower Milovaig on the far right where the Martyrs' leader John Macpherson lived.

17. GLENDALE WATER MILL

The last example left in Skye. Each of the seven parishes had two or three of these to grind the oatmeal, which, together with potatoes, was the staple food. By the side is a peat-fired kiln for drying the grain.

W1. A walk from Ramasaig to Lorgill, 1.5 miles. Lorgill (Glen of the Deer's Cry) was a township which was cleared of 10 families in 1830. The eviction notice was served in Lorgill as follows:

> 'To all the crofters in Lorgill. Take notice that you are hereby duly warned that you all be ready to leave Lorgill at 12 o'clock on the 4th of August next with all your baggage but no stock and proceed to Loch Snizort, where you will board the ship Midlothian that will take you to Nova-Scotia where you are to receive a free grant of land from Her Majesty's government. Take further notice that any crofter disobeying this order will be immediately arrested and taken to prison. All persons over 70 years of age will be taken care of in the County Poor House. This order is final and no appeal to the government will be considered'.

DUNVEGAN - PORTREE

Scenery: Moorland, sea views.

W2. Forestry walk.

Landscape story: MacLeod territory, but several estates were sold in the 1770s to meet debts. Waternish peninsula was sold in 1796 to meet further debts incurred in an unsuccessful election contest.

Crofting townships, a failed fishery village, and large estates. The road from Dunvegan to Portree was built to facilitate the cattle export trade and finished in 1811, the first road in Skye. Many prehistoric duns. Summer grazings with Norse and Gaelic names.

.

18. FAIRY BRIDGE

A natural meeting place where three valleys converge, an obvious place for buying and selling cattle from the Outer Isles, the start of that great river of black cattle that flowed down Skye to the great cattle fairs on the mainland at Falkirk and Stirling and onward to the hungry industrial and commercial centres of the south.

Free Church preachers, before they were allowed to build churches, preached here in the open.

19. STEIN (STONE)

Thomas Telford, the great engineer responsible for building the Scottish Highlands' and Skye's road network - visited here in 1790 to plan a fishery station. Harbour, storehouse and inn were built by 1797. Unfortunately, two years later the herring had gone. The inn is still here, and a little piece of street of the village that never was.

W.2 Forestry Commission walk. The car track to the forest leads off the road on the right at .3 of a mile after Stein.

20. HALLIN (SLOPING FIELD)

Hallin Old Church and Manse. You could say that Napoleon Buonaparte was responsible for much of Skye's scenery. If it had not been for the boom in cattle and kelp, would the landowners of the time have spent £200 per mile (half the cost, the government paid the other £200) on building Skye's roads, improved farms, and laid out crofting townships? And to celebrate Napoleon's defeat at Waterloo the government set aside money for Scottish churches and built Hallin and Stein churches.

Telford was engaged to produce a standard design for a church and another for the minister's house, (one or two storeys, according to circumstances) with a byre and sometimes a stable in the back of the building. Thirty two churches went up in remote highland parishes, all equipped with prefabricated metal-framed windows made in Aberdeen. Hallin Old Church and the Manse next door were finished in 1829.

21. TRUMPAN (ONE SIDED HILLOCK)

Old Church. Quite different from Telford's churches, Trumpan was built of rough stone, originally with a thatched roof. It was burnt down in Clan days together with a congregation of MacLeods inside, by a band of MacDonalds who had landed on the coast under cover of fog. Alarm beacons were lit and clan warriors from Dunvegan caught up with the MacDonalds. A fierce battle on the beach ended in a massacre of the invaders.

22. FLASHADER (FLAT SHIELING)

Summer pastures since before the Clan Period - *shader* means summer pasture in Old Norse. The hills to the south have several *shader* names. **Dun Flashader,** scanty ruins of a circular stone tower, a broch, 0.3 of a mile down the turning to Kildonan.

23. LYNDALE (VALLEY OF FLAX)

Sold off by the MacLeods in the 1770's to meet some of the £50,000 gambling and other debts run up by the 19th chief "The Wicked". The lovely woodland was planted in the 1790s when it was fashionable for landowners to improve their estates in this way.

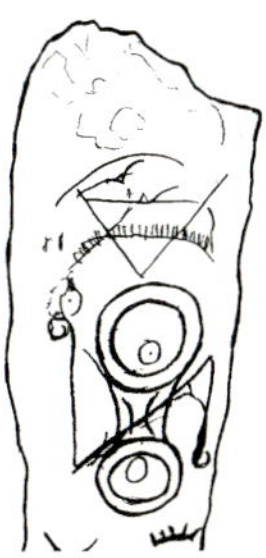

24. SKEABOST (SHELTERED LAND)

Worth a short detour 0.3 mile down the B8036 and a few hundred yards up the turn to Tote to see **Clach Ard**, a standing stone incised with mysterious symbols interpreted as commemorating a marriage with representations of a mirror and comb, made about 500 AD.

NORTH EAST

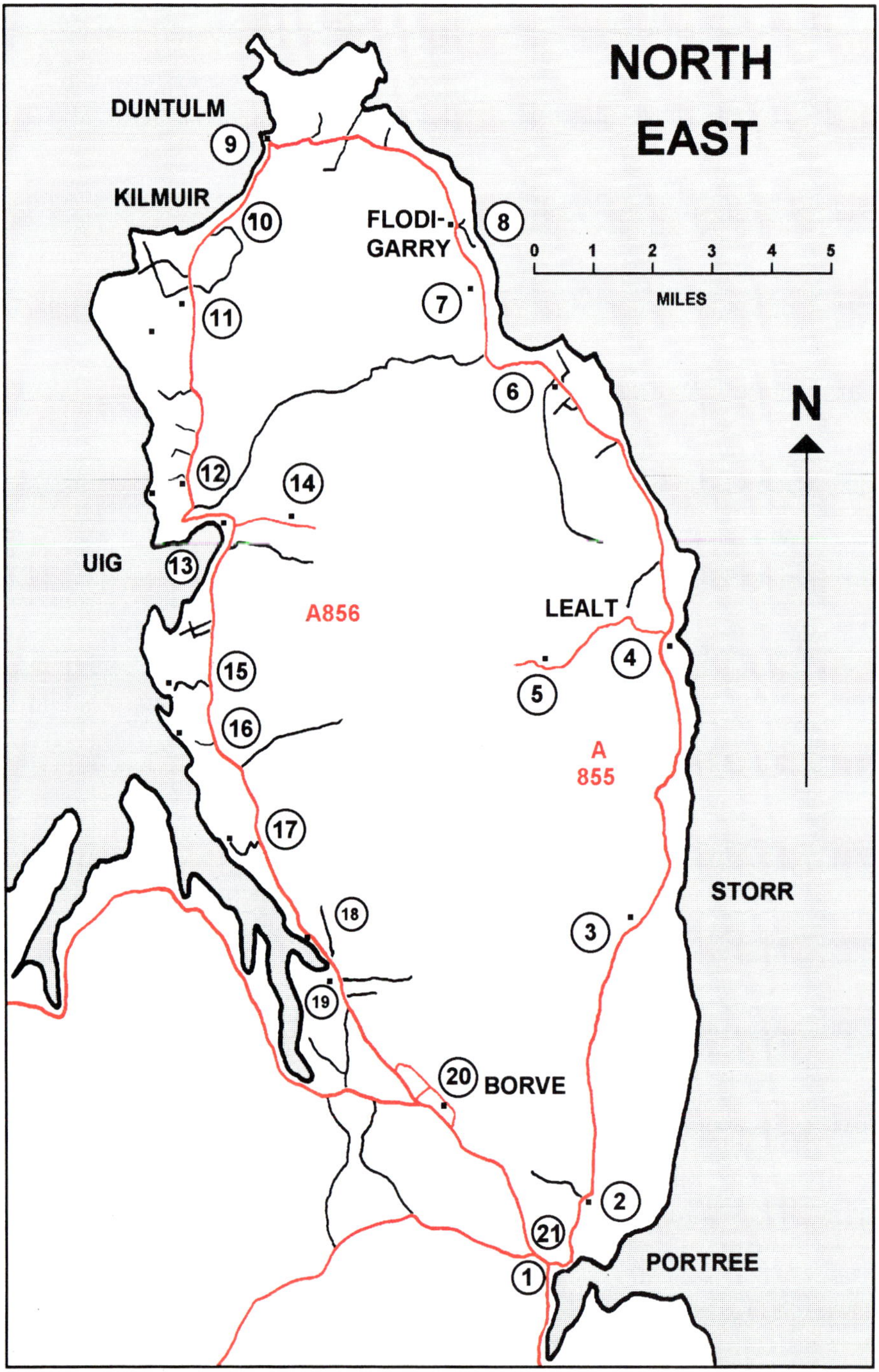
NORTH
EAST
DUNTULM
9
KILMUIR
10
FLODI-
GARRY
8
0
1
2
3
4
5
MILES
7
11
6
N
12
14
UIG
13
A856
LEALT
4
15
5
16
A
855
17
STORR
18
3
19
20
BORVE
2
21
PORTREE
1

PORTREE - STAFFIN - UIG - PORTREE

Scenery: *The extraordinary vertical cliffs of Storr and the Kilt Rock were spewed out by volcanos which erupted when Iceland split open the landmass and drifted north, about 59 million years ago.*

Landscape Story: This is the Trotternish peninsula where the land has been used for cattle and sheep since the Stone Age Neolithic farmers built their chambered tombs here around 3000BC. Ruins everywhere of Bronze and Iron Age forts show how later peoples protected themselves against raiders.

In clan times the great fortress guarding this territory was Duntulm Castle, which, with the lands, changed hands several times between the MacLeods and the MacDonalds, ending in the MacDonalds' possession and their moving up here to live, from Dunscaith castle in the south. That energetic improver, Lord MacDonald, brought the first road, to Trotternish, up to Uig in 1819, to help the cattle trade. He also laid out crofting townships. MacDonald extravagance compelled the estate's sale around 1850, and the clearances for sheep farming at that time were widely resented. The government bought the area between 1904 and 1919 and, as landlord, re-allotted it to crofters.

1. PORTREE (KING'S PORT)

In clan times when trade was by barter, with virtually no cash around, **Portree Fair** in May and August was where you would exchange your surplus oatmeal, butter, cheese, poultry, dried herring or salmon, sheep and cattle, for horses, hides, wool, or linen.

2. DUN GERASHADER

Easily seen from the Portree road, its tumbled heaps of stones crown a rocky knoll almost opposite the road to Achachork and Achtalean. A line of great boulders was once a wall surrounding the chief's dwelling, a place of refuge for his people. Typically, the dun commands a wide vista, and is worth the short climb to experience the same views as those prehistoric families did about 1000 BC. Access by a stile opposite the water scheme gateway.

3. STORR (PINNACLE)

Ten miles of empty landscape dominated by the celebrated view of the 59 million-year-old volcanic rock pillar, the Old Man of Storr. This is Scorrybreck, cleared for sheep around 1850 and turned into one sheep farm. At the head of the loch under the Storr are **lazy beds** where clansmen cultivated potatoes. Around the corner, are acres and acres of **Forestry Commission** Sitka spruce, distinguishable from Christmas trees, the Norwegian spruce, by the blue undersides of their "leaves". A small carpark enables you to park and take a walk around and through the forest. The roots of the maturing trees still grip the drainage ridges on which they were planted.

4. INVER TOTE (RUINED HOUSE)

The road takes a V bend round the River Tote and here are slopes with more **lazy beds.**

5. LEALT (HALF STREAM)

An excursion up the side road to Lealt takes you to deep prehistoric **peat banks.** As a rough rule of thumb it takes one year to lay down one millimetre of peat. In the peat there are strata of vanished woodlands so you can calculate how long ago trees flourished here. And to the south, the slopes are corrugated with a series of **lazy beds** all of which were once cultivated with the crooked spade, the *caschrom.* The road itself cuts across a raised embankment which is all that remains of the old **railway** which early this century carried out from this remote glen loads of diatomite, a light friable soil formed from algae derived from plankton.

6. STENSCHOLL (STONE SLOPE)

Kilmuir and Stenscholl Church and Manse. There are three churches here, but look for the one set back off the road. This was built with funds celebrating the defeat of Napoleon at Waterloo. Money from the victory fund was set aside to provide remote areas of the Scottish Highlands with their own church and minister's house. The designs were standardised to keep down costs. **Stenscholl church** still has its original metal frame windows prefabricated by Abernethy in Aberdeen.

The manse, a handsome Georgian house, would have stood out from the houses of the parishioners of the time. It had good chimney pieces and a mahogany stair rail. The crofters' houses were homebuilt, thatched, one-storey longhouses - the so-called blackhouses - sheltering cattle and folk under one roof, and had central peat fires without chimneys.
In those days few people had any precise idea of time. The congregation would meet in good time and the precentor would read from the scriptures whilst awaiting the minister. When he was seen approaching they would ring the bell and the people would compose themselves for the service.

7. DIGG (DITCH OR MOUND TO PROTECT FROM WATER)

One of several crofting townships laid out by the Board of Agriculture post-1904 to alleviate the land hunger in areas cleared by landlords for sheep 50 years before. In 1920 the government-sponsored Crofters' Housing Scheme accelerated the phasing-out of the old black house by providing loans and cheap building materials, specifications and plans, hence the numbers of attractive one-and-a-half storey houses with dormer or *storm* windows dating from the 1920s and 1930s.

8. FLODIGARRY (FLOATING ENCLOSURE)

Behind the hotel is **Flora MacDonald's married home** from 1750-1772. Her husband farmed here before inheriting the lease of the major clan estate at Kingsburgh on the west coast where his father had been factor, i.e. estate manager, to the MacDonald chiefs. The cottage demonstrates that, for many Skye tacksmen, the gentry of the day, their houses were small indeed.

The large building beyond, **Flodigarry Hostel,** was converted from the garages and lodgings which housed the Rolls Royces and their chauffeurs serving the guests at the hotel between the wars.

9. DUNTULM (FORT ON THE CLIFF)

Built above sheer cliffs, **Duntulm Castle** was formerly a prehistoric stronghold as the "dun" element of the name implies. In clan days coast-watchers were always stationed in the windows. Underneath these were the menacing barrels of the cannons. The traitorous clansman Hugh the Clerk was imprisoned in a dungeon here, given salt meat and left to die of thirst.

10. KILMUIR (MARY'S CHURCH)

The chief building of the **Museum of Island Life** is a croft house built in 1904; the museum depicts life of that period and afterwards. It has the typical box-beds, one hung with locally grown and woven red linen curtains. Originally three houses, the site now comprises seven, showing different aspects of crofting life.

11. KILMUIR, KILVAXTER (CHURCH OF THE BAKER) LINICRO (FLAX ENCLOSURE) BALGOWN (TOWN OF THE SMITH)

String of **townships,** laid out with crofts c1904 by the Board of Agriculture as on the east coast, see Digg above.

12. SKUDDABORG (SMALL NEIGHBOURING HAMLETS)

Below the **viewpoint** here lies a great shallow bowl of land which was once a loch with an island housing a monastery of tiny stone beehive-shape cells built by the Irish monks, the followers of St Columba. It was drained by Lord MacDonald, he who owned both Trotternish in the north and the Sleat peninsula in the south.
In the centre of the view are the ruins of the MacDonalds' house of **Monkstadt** built with stone shipped from the ruins of their castle at Duntulm. Here the fugitive Prince Charles was entertained, disguised as Flora MacDonald's maid. He nearly gave the game away when keeping his skirts dry, fording a river.
The ruins of **Dun Skudiburgh** can just be seen on the coastline to the south on a rocky knoll. This was built around 500 BC for a local chief. Ruins of a wall 3m. thick surround its defensive tower, well-placed to keep watch for seaborne raiders. To visit it, approach it along the coast at low tide to avoid the farm land.

13. UIG (BAY)

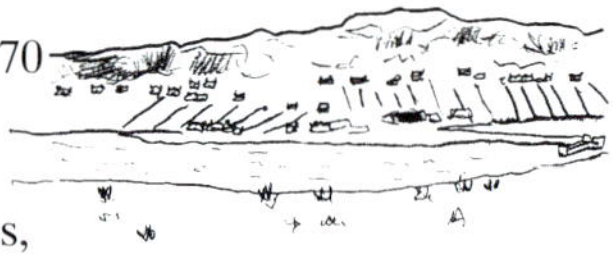

High above Uig Bay in one of the most picturesque of situations, 70 **crofts** were laid out by Lord MacDonald around 1815. Old photographs of the 1880s show old blackhouses where now are white painted modern homes and the present day crofts, now grass, would have been striped with different crops, hay, oats, potatoes, turnips.

14. CONON (GENTLE FLOWING RIVER)

Worth a detour up this narrow and steep road for the view of Conon Wood in the gorge, a relict of Skye's **ancient woodland,** and for a glimpse of **Conon**, a township in an alpine-like valley. Each house lies next to its original freestone predecessor built when the Board of Agriculture bought the estate to divide into crofts in 1904.

15. CUIDRACH (PLACE OF POWER)

Bestowed by the MacDonald chief on a famous warrior turned cattle-dealer, Do' MacIain ic Shearmuis, who, with a fearsome reputation as a swordsman, was able to pioneer cattle-droving to Falkirk through the lawless highlands of the 1600s. He once saved the life of his son-in-law who sought refuge with him after killing a MacAlister in a drunken brawl. The sight of this man patrolling the door with his long sword drawn was enough to make the pursuit decide it was safer to leave him alone.

Before the grant of Cuidrach, Do' MacIain's claims to an estate had been overlooked. One day he was entertaining the clan chief's bard (he was a fine poet himself) who was shocked at the neglect of a fellow poet. On his return to the chief's court he took advantage of the traditional freedom of a bard to express his opinion and declaimed a scathing poem on this injustice, not ceasing until the chief agreed to settle land on Do' MacIain.

16. SOUTH CUIDRACH

Caisteal Uisden, Hugh's castle, was built by a treacherous MacDonald and possibly was never lived in. Hugh planned to murder the chief and his entourage at a house-warming celebration but mixed up the invitation with plot instructions to his confederates. Captured by the redoubtable Do' MacIain, (see above) he died in a dungeon at Duntulm, (see Duntulm above). Hugh's castle, built soon after 1600, was a massive rectangular tower with walls over two metres thick. To visit the ruins which are substantial, take the farm track to South Cuidrach, park at the gate and walk to the farm steadings from where a track leads to the castle.

17. KINGSBURGH,

Another estate formerly held by senior members of the clan. Flora MacDonald's father in law lived at **Kingsburgh** and was imprisoned for his part in the 1745 Rebellion. He was factor for the clan estates, and held in high regard. It was said of him, "So long as a spark of honesty remains, the name of MacDonald of Kingsburgh will ever have a mark of veneration put upon it". His eldest son Allan, husband of Flora, was the very flower of a Highland gentleman in strength and looks. He was also the best judge of cattle in his day, and much in demand at this time when cattle formed a major part of the rents. Allan drove many a herd to the cattle fairs of Falkirk

18. KINSALEYRE

Two standing stones, survivors of what folk memory says were many circles and stones in the area which were removed to facilitate farming around the late 1700s, these are easily visible from the road. **19. Chambered Cairn,** drive into the church park for a good view across the moor of this prehistoric tomb.

20. BORVE

A short detour along the hill to Borve, the five s**tanding stones** aligned in a cross set you wondering what astral significance they may once have had. Circles and stones were set out with sophisticated precision to coincide with seasonal movements of the sun, moon and stars around 1700 BC.

21. PORTREE CATTLE STANCE

The trysting ground was about three-quarters of a mile outside Portree to the northwest. Said John MacCullough in 1824:

'Do not pay it a visit, when all sorts of cattle come to be bought and sold; when horn is entangled in horn, and drover with drover.' and of the inn - 'Have I not sat over the fumes of tobacco amid the steam of hot whiskey to listen to prices and bone and rib and weight and pedigree till I could almost have bought and sold a stot myself...And therefore I took refuge from the Lairds and Chiefs in the opener element of the fair itself. And then the cows, and the queys, and the stots, and the stirks, began to bellow and roar, and whisk their tails, and the sellers of cows and the buyers of cows began to compete for the mastery and all the town began to look like a stable, and I had nothing to do but to leave them to poke about their horns and bellow down the Highland drovers if they could, or remain to be daubed by the whisking of the cows' tails in Portree itself'.

Index of Place Names